Breath For A Weary Soul

Lynn Parker

© Copyright 2016 by Lynn Parker

All rights reserved. No part of this collection may be reproduced or transmitted in any form or by any means, electronic or mechanical, including photocopying and recording, or by any information storage and retrieval system, except in the case of brief quotations for use in articles and reviews, without written permission from the author.

This is an original work. Some of the names, characters, places and incidents are real, others are fictitious—the product of the author's imagination. Any resemblance to actual persons not identified specifically is entirely coincidental.

7710-T Cherry Park Dr, Ste 224
Houston, TX 77095
713-766-4271

Paperback: 978-1-68411-072-8

Table of Contents

Divine Design　　　　　　　　　　　　5

1. What Were The Chances?
2. In The Field
3. The Keeper
4. And Remember
5. My Father
6. If Not, Then Who?
7. Chase Hard After Me!
8. Curtain's Lifting
9. There Was A Crucifixion
10. A Toast

Inspiration/ Encouragement　　　　　27

1. A Long Time To Get Here
2. Jolene's Kitchen
3. Escape From "WAS"
4. Everything I Had
5. Could I Dare To Dream?
6. Without Spot Or Wrinkle
7. A Whistle
8. Caskets Or Cocoons?
9. It Is Finished!
10. Surrender Of An Only Son

Reflections on The 21st Century   **149**

1. Babble On In Babylon
2. Locked Up Or Dead!
3. Do You Have Flowers?
4. From Scratch
5. Last One Standing
6. In Spite Of
7. Howl At The Moon
8. Stand Down
9. Snipers On Those Hills
10. The Heartland

Divine Design

WHAT WERE THE CHANCES?

My husband sat peacefully sleeping in the easy chair in our living room. He was blissfully unaware that I was smiling at him, as he snored loudly enough, to periodically wake himself up. I marveled at the road I had taken to meet this man who now shared my life.

As I reflected on the improbability of our meeting and the even greater unlikelihood of marital harmony that would weather life together, I saw the miracle of our union.

I began to contemplate what the chances were that our lives would have ever intersected; the chances of our connecting, and the chances of our moving forward inextricably joined together by a promise.

Hence the impetus that fueled this musing.

What were the chances, the odds you might say,
That you'd have found me and be married today?
What were the chances we'd somehow have found,
That soul mate, that helpmate, that perfection all 'round?

What were the chances that east could meet west,
That yin could meet yang and be happily blessed?
What were the chances after all these long years,
We'd still be together, through laughter and tears?

AND...

What were the chances that life would wield blows,
That hit us blindsided, spilling us head over toes?
What were the chances we'd have made it through strife;
Some kicking, some clawing, some holding on for dear life?

What were the chances that as each of us grew,
You'd still like me, and by luck, I'd like you?
What were the chances we'd have jostled so long,
That we finally got comfy, in fact, we belong?

What were the chances we'd ever get passed,
Those bitsy nitpickings to find peace that would last?
What were the chances that we'd see tough times through;
And gaze on in wonder a new me, and new you?

Dumb luck may claim some, coincidence few;
But add it, divide it, extrapolate too.
You must simply conclude it's not up for debate,
Our marriage is more than mere karma or fate.

YOU SEE...

Mathematically speaking, chance couldn't explain
Why we didn't turn tail at the first sign of rain.
My guess is it isn't by luck we still stand,
But by grace, and the mercy of the Master's right hand!

What were the chances He'd have brought us safe through;
And molded and stretched us, and transformed us too?
It couldn't have been by chance after all,
Or we'd still be light headed, black and blue from the fall.

He took two young kids without half a clue,
And battled 'long side us with His vision in view.
Are we how He imagined? Perhaps not just yet,
But if chance enters in, I'll be placing my bet.

There still may be wrestling, and tumbling, and tears;
Good times and laughter, and nightmarish years.
My prayer is that God will look down from above,
And guide us and keep us in His perfect love!

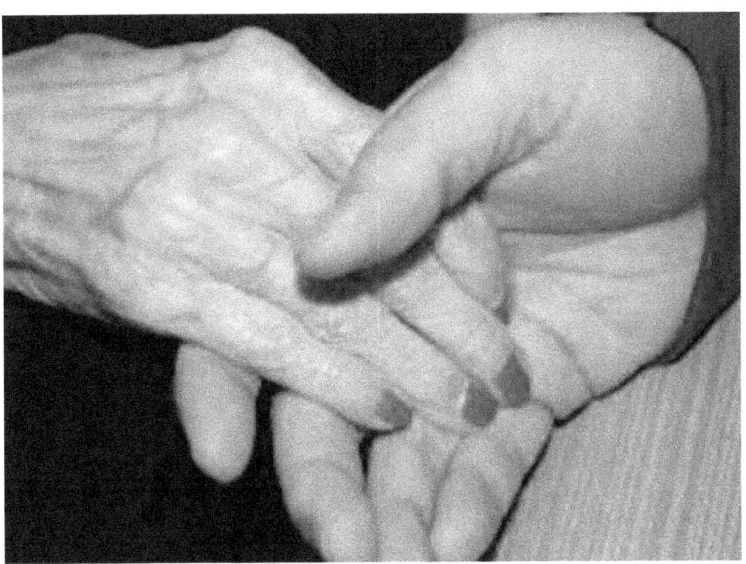

IN THE FIELD

This poem is a celebration of all that God has created. It is a celebration of His Son Jesus who came to seek and save those who are lost. We can open our eyes each day and marvel at the variety and complexity of this world, and rest securely knowing that He cares for us. We can say of His creation, as He unabashedly did—"It is very good!"

Nothing of note, 'bout an acre square,
Was the field on the east divide.
It was little more than a drainage bowl,
With a dam on the farthest side.

Thick woods were a frame, mostly oaks and pines,
And the shinnery made the going tough.
But it was worth the toil when the wind was right,
To find a place on the northern bluff.

No telling what you'd see from that vantage point,
If your movements were measured and slow.
To catch nature, unaware, in their commonplace,
And to watch them in that field below.

There was no way to tell, from a quick first glance,
The richness of that acre square.
But I loved to watch as the treetops flushed,
And marveled at the multitudes right there.

Once at dusk, as the light ebbed low,
And a reddish golden hue was everywhere;
A fox trotted out, moving left to right,
Seeming as if he danced on air.

And the golden dusk lit his tail aflame,
And the redness of his coat a silver blaze.
I sat back in awe, still and breathless at the scene.
Could close my eyes and picture it for days.

If you had the chance to be early on the bluff,
In the fall when the air turned cool,
The ducks and geese gave an aerial display,
As they frolicked in the runoff pool.

The masked raccoon sipped at the shallow end,
And the possum brought her brood from up the tree.
As they tumbled out, she'd lift her nose to scent.
Must admit it was quite a sight to see.

And an eagle soared, and from his vantage point,
Gave a solitary cry through miles of air,
And the sun reflected off his feathered crown,
A view of splendor prompting all to stare.

The pinnacle of joy was to glimpse that buck,
To watch his stately entrance in the field.
Much too wise to stay in the clear for long,
Fall's the only time his caution has to yield.

I have watched him grow; seen those massive tines
Fill out thicker, longer, wider every year.
Seen his girth rotund; seen him stand mature.
Any hunter would be proud to claim that deer.

You have a field, *it's your life,* my friend,
And if you stop just long enough, you'll see,
That what you thought was barren ground
will spring alive before your eyes.
It holds treasures for a heart set free!

THE KEEPER

The funeral was a celebration of a life well-lived. Her grandson gave a testimony about how she had kept him after school. That she had treasured his finger paintings, and newspaper sports clippings.

He ended his tribute to her by saying that she herself was "A keeper." She became what she was: "A keeper!"

That description left me thinking about our Heavenly Father, who is our Keeper. He is The Keeper of everything. Hence this poem.

He is The Keeper of the store;
Though none for sale the treasures that He holds.
Sweet tears and dreams; new mercies never sold.
He is The Keeper of the store.

He is The Keeper of the score.
No vengeful plot need occupy thy mind.
Hold thy course! …thy tongue! …thy peace to find.
He is The Keeper of the score.

He is The Keeper of the gate.
His throngs keep watch to usher home His own.
You'll not see heaven but through Him alone.
He is The Keeper of the gate.

He is The Keeper of all time.
Unerring hand through all eternity.
Fear not the way, though dark it may well be.
He is The Keeper of all time.

He is The Keeper of thy soul.
Rest long, secure He shall not stop to sleep.
But guard thy way, and beckon deep's call unto deep.
He is The Keeper of thy soul.

He is The Keeper!

AND REMEMBER

The enemy of God's people has long battled to take captives or to captivate. His wicked plot is to distract us long enough to destroy us—to lure us away or veer us off track until we are lost in the muck and mire of this world. It is the battle of a lifetime to keep his evil designs at bay. Victory over the schemes of our enemy requires constant focus.

The Healer of our souls, our Lord Jesus Christ, must remain at the forefront of our minds so that in all life's ebbs and flows we can say that "we are more than conquerors;" that with Him "all things are possible," and that "if He is for us who is it that can come against us" successfully?

This poem is meant as an encouragement for those who have been carried far afield. Who either have believed evil held no real danger, or by being "sucker punched" in some season of life—have taken their eyes, however briefly, off the one and only Jesus! We have lived to tell our story.

Days can pass with peace and sweet surrender.
At times "just cause" can spawn a war.
I turn again to see You unmatched. Tender.
Hints of joy that heaven has in store.

Inside my heart I long for mount top splendor.
Far from toil and valley's dampened gloom.
To know my dreams come from the Truest Sender,
Gives breath to life inside this lonely tomb.

I trust the One who rules. Supreme Defender!
Builds in us every tool that is required.
Sometimes the Judge! Sometimes the soothing Mender!
Tender shoot—be formed and fashioned—tempered! Fired!

While all things work through Him—for good to render.
When dark attacks the mind and steals the peace.
I lay me down! "Stock still!" and will remember…
"Fear not!" The balm that brings release.

MY FATHER

This poem is simply a praise to our Father, who deserves all glory! When we take an inventory of His handiwork we cannot reasonably conclude that this marvelous planet could have been created in any other way than by Him. Chaos could never have given birth to order! The rhythm and the rhyme of our world could not have just happened. Everything in this universe points back to the Creator. His creation bears His fingerprint unmistakably!

My Father owns the cattle
On a thousand emerald hills.
He charts the river's fractured course
'Til over roaring falls it spills.

My Father whispers to the fowl,
"'Tis time, take flight and soar!
Follow the sky's predestined paths
Where your fathers flew before!"

My Father commands the waves to calm,
Says to the wind, "Be Still!"
He maps the ocean's ebb and flow;
A time to empty and refill.

In spring, my Father plants the seeds
And waters carefully.
Grass comes forth, and myrtle blooms,
Cool shade of stately tree.

My Father speaks and mountains move;
Tells sun to rise just so!
He orchestrates vast galaxies;
Crafts starry night light's glow.

My Father blankets earth in white,
And mercifully says, "Rest."
And creatures sleep, too—fallowed fields;
As my Father has behest.

My Father's wisdom does provide
Sage words—Creation's Creed!
To cease from toil, restock, restore,
And silo season's seed.

My Father sees with eagle's eye,
And pierces hearts of stone.
He knows the treacherous road we take;
Can translate each tear-drenched moan.

Crawl up into my Father's lap
And let your guard fall fast.
My Father's power commands the storm;
His rule forever lasts.

My Father sees each season change;
For eons His purview.
No mere chance or idle gaffe
Can make His Word untrue.

Behold my Father makes all things
Brand new as is His choice.
Stand still! Take note, and tarry not
When at last you hear His voice!

IF NOT, THEN WHO?

Creation is a testament to the reality and presence of an Almighty God. Creation is merely His calling card; a sample of the breadth of His majesty, and the genius of His glorious essence.

We can look out over God's handiwork on this globe and marvel at the uniqueness of His creative design. We can ponder how any other rational explanation could be formulated to explain the genesis of earth's precise consistent patterns and intricate balances.

With careful scientific study, it seems impossible to conclude that the world around us could have randomly happened. Could it have been a mere serendipity, or an accidental cosmic alignment?

The statistical improbability of order coming out of chaos, further complicated by its reliably repeating itself down to the minutest detail, leaves little wiggle room for any other theory to explain creation's origin.

There is much documented empirical evidence that supports a creator; negating even the most honest skeptic's supposition of some other viable cause for the functioning cosmos today. This world could not have occurred by chance.

If a sunrise leaves you much impressed.
If the blinding colors bursting forth attest.
If the spectacle you see, gives you not one clue,
Of the painter's genius stroking every hue.
If man surely could not birth a day,
If not him, then who?

If an azure sky elicits pause.
If the panoramic view seems to hold no flaws.
If the vast expanse of an endless blue,
Gives not one hint of just how it grew.
Since man could not create the sky,
If he could not, then who?

If a child's laughter causes all to smile.
If their games prove that toil can be left a while.
If their voices urge, "Come, *you* play too!"
And tug upon your apron 'till in fact, you do.
If man could not fathom how to birth pure joy,
If not man, then who?

If a plan had been handed down through time.
That called for forgiveness of a debt all mine.
If another paid the bill; let no penalty accrue,
And by that act of sacrifice came *life* brand new.
If man had no power to redeem, save one.
Had Jesus not, once for all, then who?

CHASE HARD AFTER ME!

A logical person, who would look into the vastness and variety of things that incorporate our universe, would have to conclude that the intricacy and harmony that rules the galaxies could not be accidental, but were planned in refined detail.

If there is a plan, then there must be a planner. God is the Architect of creation. He has given testimony to the workings of His Hands by the presence of order over chaos; the fashioning of time by calendars, clocks, and the cosmos. He prescribes justice and metes out judgment. He offers forgiveness and bestows blessings.

His plan has been in place since before the beginning and has been executed throughout the ages with impeccable perfection. Graciously, now and then He opens a window to the mystery of Himself and allows mankind to peek inside to receive wisdom and revelation.

Without a divine spark, there is no explaining where love and laughter emanate from. Without His godly wiring, we are incapable of feeling the full measure of life's pure emotion; leaving us to imitate His essence with pharmaceuticals and adrenaline rushes. Those who cannot acknowledge the fine-tuned excellence of creation are left to ask the question, "What is the point of life anyway?"

The genesis of this poem came from the pastor who stood before me, whose words came at me like a bolt of electricity. He said, "It was as if God put the key to 'me' in

His coat pocket and started up the mountain; and as He climbed, He turned back to me and said, 'If you want to know who you are, chase Me!'"

Those remarkable pastor's words were the impetus that gave birth to this poem.

If there's a time unfolding, and a purpose etched in stone;
If there's a place of entrance, and a season yet unknown.
If there can be no accident to what seems a mystery,
Our Father plants the seed in us then bids,
"Follow faithfully."

If there is no randomness to life as it unveils;
If there's a charted map for each, laid out in grand detail.
If we dare to set a course, though hard it may well be,
Our Father, who holds the key to us, shouts,
"Chase hard after Me!"

If the mantra of this world falls faint on tender ears;
If the promises long tested, prove true throughout the years.
Then sure as God gives life a breath, and fashions every trial,
His Word stands firm thoughtout all time,
Invites respite every mile.

If we can know without a doubt, who moves the galaxies;
That an Architect with mastery has created flawlessly.
Then the aching that's unspoken, buried deep that none can see,
Most certainly finds healing as He whispers,
"Chase hard after Me."

Should a season tempt your heart to faint and question, how or why;
If your reasoning gives no comfort, and all hope begins to die.
If the day brings burdens plenty, steals all light and energy;
Know God has power to bear the load, for all eternity.

Look up to where your hope comes from; where power and peace reign true.
He knows the way you take this day; has victory's end in sight for you.
He is the One who made you, knows your purpose, who you'll be.
Lift up your eyes and heed His call,
"Chase hard after Me!"

CURTAIN'S LIFTING

The Book of Revelation, the last book in the Christian Bible, holds many prophetic predictions that will unfold at the end of the Church Age, as the millennial reign of Christ is ushered in, and God's Kingdom is established on earth.

The author of Revelation, the apostle John, while exiled on an inhospitable island, was privileged to receive an escort through heaven. Jesus assured him that a time was coming on the Kingdom calendar when all wrongs would be made right. A Champion for truth and justice would descend from on high, and a battle would take place to reclaim for all time, Christ's rightful place on the throne.

As we witness the events of this book play out in world events today, we can rest assured that they are unfolding as they were foretold. The cast of players in the last days were foreknown, and none of the current happenings are catching God unaware or ill-prepared.

His Kingdom is advancing unencumbered by the wiles of the devil and his minions. One day, in the fullness of time, heaven's books will be opened and the record will be set straight. This poem is a reflection of this assurance.

Draw back the curtain and gaze full screen;
Hear the edicts! What can this mean?
Some wild-eyed half-wit must surely be;
Telling frightening tales—spinning yarns! You'll see!

But wait! Who wrote? 'Twas the disciple John;
The one most loved, has somehow seen beyond!
He wrote, *"In the beginning was the Word;*
He was God, and was with God!" Sounds quite absurd.

John laid the framework and built the case;
How God's own Son walked through this place.
John had rested his head, heard Divine heart's beat;
Felt the shaking ground 'neath Golgotha's feet.

He had seen the tombstone rolled away;
Seen too, the nail scars on display.
So, 'tis not odd that in old age;
On Patmos Isle, John penned sure page.

And captured the vision as best he could;
From Heaven's halls where his spirit stood.
Ablaze with questions, quizzed angelic guide;
Awestruck with wonder, as each seal's untied.

Types and shadows meld seamlessly;
Perfected plan. Matchless Deity!
Can John be trusted? Can this one who weaves?
Can he be a beacon, if a heart will believe?

Trust the one who saw the Son;
Watched His life on earth, and the life to come!
"Hark, true words!" comes herald's plea.
Let hearers hear, and seers see!

The curtain lifts, unveiled future known;
Come Faithful Rider, reclaim your own!

THERE WAS A CRUCIFIXION

For some, it is hard to grapple with the idea that the existence of evil does not preclude the presence of God. Some conclude that because bad things happen in this world, there must be no God. This is tragically flawed logic, based on the fact that people can simply open their eyes and see that this universe, with all its seamless complexities, could not be a product of chance.

As we embrace the plan of God, not only for all of mankind throughout all ages, but for ourselves in this age, we must understand that God will work into us, out of us, and through us, everything He has purposed for us. What is required appears, at times, to be unbelievably cruel. But, should we opt to trust God, and believe His promises even though the road ahead of us seems black as night, we will become all He created us to be.

Not much depth of character can be molded into the life that never faces adversity; that never has to dig deep into its own internal well of fortitude and move through a trying season of life with perseverance. If our plan is to venture forth in this world, praying that no storms come, no losses happen, no pain overshadows, how foolish to think we would become all we are supposed to be.

Patience, wisdom, kindness, goodness, gratefulness, and the like, cannot be fashioned in a life without testing or trials. We can trust God to create something better in us through every hardship. We can rest secure in the knowledge that He is not cruel by nature, and that there is an expected good end for every trial endured. Life is not always good or fair, but "God works in all things" and will use even the tragedies of our lives for good.

There was a place on Calvary's hill,
Where men looked on, hushed witness 'til,
The hammer swung, pinned hands, pierced feet,
Sin raised Him up…the task complete!

And ruled the Savior "a charlatan."
Man's justice ruled, thought "right" had won.
The blasphemer claimed He was God's Son.
He'd reaped His fate; His hour had come!

Creation mourned, a fate foreknown!
There was foretold a coming crucifixion.

What happened next would testify.
The sun went black, so too, the sky!
The trembling earth, creation groaned.
God's wrath held back, yet confirmed His Own.

And reckoned to men He was no fraud.
He'd told the truth, the Son of God!
Devilish force lost all that day.
Fiery lake ahead, prepare to pay!

Wicked lot, the fate forecast;
After all, there'd been a crucifixion.

In life He put no trust in man.
With steel resolve, advanced God's plan.
And took no thought for rank nor power,
But bowed His will and embraced cruel hour.

He summoned no angelic force.
Sought freedom's victory. Stood firm, on course!
Nor rallied He from Heaven's throne.
The trump was still, the Lamb atoned!

Full well He knew for Abram was,
There'd have to be a crucifixion!

Beware the urge, when facing pain,
To hatch own plan to advance again.
Your faint heart's choice to skirt hard date.
Eat the candy. Perennially full, the plate!

Be sure you'll find the valley road,
Where sky goes black and harsh the goad.
But by His stripes our healing's sure!
Lift up your cross! Battle cry, "Endure!"

Though it cost every precious thing you own;
There must be, after all, a crucifixion.

For there is a prize beyond our view,
Where peace abounds; and all things are new!
But it does not come with pauper's buy.
The cost? Your life! "Yourself" must die.

And from the ashes, beauty's found.
Let go the things that held high ground.
That entertained, and kept you vexed.
He "IS" the way beyond what's next!

Your loss is gain! To Him be true.
Your resurrection's birthed on the hill of crucifixion.

A TOAST

The following is a celebration of all things furry and four-legged. God has given us the most wonderful of gifts... the love of an animal. Statistics bear out what all pet owners instinctively know. A pet will keep you healthier and happier longer.

This is a toast to honor those pets who fill our lives and steal our hearts.

Here's to muddy paws on sofa cushions, and
Dancing feet for safe homecomings.
Here's to contrite looks for stolen socks and
Mistakes made in hallways.

Here's to wet noses and wetter kisses.
Here's to toenails tapping on tile floors.
Here's to caverns dug in prized gardens,
For uprooted pots, the former home of some tender morsel.

Here's to rocks gathered, and squirrels treed.
Here's to bones eaten with great relish and
Buried snacks unearthed when planting pansies in the fall.
Here's to frog and snail inspections and barking escorts for
Terrapin travelers who dare to enter the yard.

Here's to the complex language of a bark,
Which transmits all manner of trouble.
Here's to creative dance moves choreographed
To express, "My food bowl is empty daddy!"

Here's to heart stopping howls that signal
Matters of national security--after all…
"The plumber is in the driveway mommy!"
Here's to stalwart chaperones sitting bedside for days
When you have the flu.

Here's to tails thumping enthusiastically
When the treat jar lid jingles open.
Here's to grey muzzles and arthritic hips
And shorter walks around the neighborhood.

Here's to snuggles on cold winter nights and
Snores that rival inbound trains.
Here's to looks of pure ecstasy
When tummies are rubbed or haunches are scratched.

and…

Here's to old men and older women,
Whose hearts are freely given, and
Who can confess unabashedly, through tears
And trembling voices ….

"I LOVED THAT DOG! "

Inspiration & Encouragement

A LONG TIME TO GET HERE

I heard a sage voice claim that youth is wasted on the young. I can attest to the truth of that statement. Wisdom, for me, came via the school of hard knocks, that was years in the making. How tragic it was to spend a life chasing an elusive dream and miss living in the process! How gracious of God to reveal the folly of such an imbalanced pursuit and to give me divine insight into His plan for me. He has a plan for each of His children. We are not accidents! We were created for a purpose that, uniquely, only we are designed to complete properly.

If we miss that purpose, we shortchange those whose lives we were meant to impact and we rob God of the glory He would have received. There is wisdom in taking stock of where we are headed, and folly if we fail to redirect our focus when we sense God's prompting.

May no one who reads this poem continue to chart a course of their own. Rather, let each look to God for true direction. It is folly to subscribe to the misconception that we are all captains of our own ships and masters of our own souls. God's Word tells quite a different story. He is both the Author and Finisher of our faith!

I carried the weight of the world so it seemed,
Hard labor each step of the way.
Unwilling to drop not the tiniest bit,
And lighten the load just one day.

Casting my burdens on Him, though He urged,
Was too foreign for me to adhere.
Engulfed in the end, had no choice, must concede,
It took a long time to get me to here.

A somber death march, and endurance test trudge,
Was my view of each dawning of day.
Had no light-hearted gait; never kicked up my heels,
Never saw any joy 'long the way.

Weeping may be for a night, so His claimed,
But my nights were just tear after tear.
'Til light shone through the black, lit a flame in the dark.
It took a long time to get me to here.

"Worry," my constant companion, held court,
In my mind it fueled fretting and doubt.
"What if's" set up camp, and held me by force,
Convinced me there was no way out!

I came to bring life, and abundantly so,
Was His promise to battle my fear.
As I clung to Him tight, began claiming lost ground.
It took a long time to get me to here.

Feeling hard-pressed to fit; to be one of the bunch,
Forfeiting all semblance of tact.
Ever blinding conformed, buying lies, fed more lore.
Never dividing pure fiction from fact.

My Spirit in you will lead to all truth,
Was His edict 'fore leaving this sphere.
Mining truth like lost gold; narrow path, marked and sure.
It took a long time to get me to here.

What I used to mark "normal" now seems so passé,
And up-side is down without doubt.
Cowed into silence! Mum is the word,
No questions allowed or you're out.

He came for the captive, His sweetest love song,
To make all things new. Never fear!
Was once counted lost, wretched soul found new life,
It took a long time to get me to here.

So, what's worthy of standing your ground on this day,
To dig in your heels and protest?
To fight for the absolute truth in this life,
To sacrifice good for the best!

Laboring, lumbering, bemoaning the fate,
Of a world growing darker each year.
Long road, hard fought ground. Counted cost, standing firm!
It took a long time to get me to here.

JOLENE'S KITCHEN

This poem is an ode to a great woman of God who was the creator of an herb farm in East Texas. She is my husband's aunt and one of my all-time favorite people. She has sage counsel for those of us who care to listen to the stories of her life, which now have tipped over the ninety years "high water mark" on the calendar. She has seen the horse and buggy days, as well as a man land on the moon. She has known happiness and her own share of grief.

Her name is Kathryn. This story holds a special memory for me. It tells of a day when far more than sauerkraut making took place. Her friend Jolene now owns her old kitchen, but the life Kathryn lived at the herb farm, called Holly Hill, still holds her heart.

We started up the private drive,
Auntie wheeling, with me beside.
We had a date and we were late,
To make "kraut" in Jolene's kitchen.

The road wound east and then turned west,
Parking spot by the sign marked "Guest."
We were loaded down, cobbled path around,
Up the stairs to Jolene's kitchen.

The house sat high, a butter hue,
With whitewashed porch and gazebo too.
Friends greeted us, made the sweetest fuss,
And led the way to Jolene's kitchen.

Counting cabbages big as bowling balls.
By Auntie's count, there were nine in all.
We began to pare and then despair,
We'd made a mess of Jolene's kitchen.

We chopped and churned added salt and sweet,
Packed canning jars, the job complete.
Then found a broom and swept the room,
Trying to tidy Jolene's kitchen.

A mount of kraut was made that day.
Divided up, we were on our way.
A memory store, tender thoughts galore,
Of that day in Jolene's kitchen.

But I have not told the true reveal,
Auntie's sadness, her heart concealed.
With grace she walks, and seldom talks,
'Bout her days in Jolene's kitchen.

The place had been her dream you see,
Labored hard my sweet Auntie.
Came Holly Hill life's blood until,
Not hers, but Jolene's kitchen.

She spoke in quiet tones and told,
Of memories true, her cherished gold.
Jack's last days near fire ablaze,
The legacy of Jolene's kitchen.

Precious the day, even more an hour,
Seasons bloom, waft scented flower.
Will come a time, when life sublime,
Brings another to Jolene's kitchen.

Weeping comes and we endure,
Seasons change keeping motives pure.
A harvest ripe, some new delight,
Will be birthed in Jolene's kitchen.

ESCAPE FROM "WAS"

This poem is a testimony to the power of Christ in any life. If you can find the courage to cry out to Him, no matter where you are in life, He will not forsake you! He is our way out of the dark and into the marvelous light.

Abraham left Ur one day,
And Dorothy woke from Oz,
And I proclaim with happy heart,
That I escaped from "WAS."

I spent many years in "WAS" you know,
With head held high and spirit low.
All seemed in place, pure window dress,
Half-hearted smiles amid distress.

It seemed so safe, such normalcy,
To pretend perfection on some quiet sea.
Yet knowing all was not quite well;
Searing pain, but dared not tell.

Laugh a little on waves of tears,
Self-loathing grows and so too, fears.
They'll like me if I'll just be more...
Rejection pounced at my front door.

"Stop the madness, please let me go!"
I cried on bended knee.
That's when He came, my Savior strong,
And gently lifted me...

Into His arms and held me close,
And stroked my tear drenched hair.
"Did you think I'd left you?" He softly asked.
"Did you think I didn't care?"

"I've watched you fight for all these years,"
He said with the sweetest voice.
"You've soldiered on a wounded soul,
But I came to give you choice."

"Choose life this day." He whispered strong,
"You don't belong in 'WAS.'
You are my own, I've come for you.
I tell you this because...

"I have a plan for you," He said.
"Get up, get on your way!
Take on new life; regain your strength,
Get up and seize the day!"

"'WAS' has merely crippled you,
Convinced you of your dearth.
'WAS' picked you clean, and left you bare,
'WAS' claimed you have no worth."

"Not true! Not true! It is a lie!"
He shouted to my heart.
"You're my delight, my pride and joy,
You deserve a brand new start."

"Forget about this place called 'WAS,'
And the hold it has on you.
Forget the torment, tears, and pain
That 'WAS' has put you through."

"You're free from all 'WAS' says you are,
From hurt, and pride, and shame.
From false illusions, guilt, and fear,
From taking all the blame."

"No longer bound, the gate's unlocked,
Step free into the light!
Hold fast to Him, life's surest Guide,
The Way, the Truth, the Life.

It may seem strange, though freed from "WAS,"
And free I claim to be.
That every now and then, by rote,
I travel back to see.

Not by choice, but habits strong,
and hauntings fraught with doubt.
"WAS" has not changed! But thankfully…
I have God's roadmap out!

EVERYTHING I HAD

This poem is my testimony. I had dreamt of being a professional golfer from a very young age, and spent most of my life in the pursuit of that dream. I had a preconceived idea that reaching the pinnacle of professional ladies golf would make me feel a certain way; an idea that, sadly, was, for me, not the reality. It was not the fault of the tour. It was, rather, that my preconception was much different than the experience. The life of a professional golfer was not what I had dreamt it would be.

The truth of that, was a letdown that cut me to the core; a devastating blow, a mourning more accurately characterized. I had worked toward this goal since early childhood, and now I was faced with a cold hard truth that I may have wasted my life and frittered away my energy in a pursuit that would never match my passion, or satisfy my ambition.

Seeing my dream evaporate, left me lost for a long time. Without a Plan B I felt adrift in the world; floating through the days and years, with little hope and little left that captivated my imagination. That is, until Jesus found me and breathed life into me again! He gave me "beauty for ashes," and a "garment of praise, instead of a spirit of heaviness." In truth, He rescued me!

These words were penned to encourage someone who may be experiencing something similar, a nagging regret for an ill-chosen path, for a dream that capsized, or for a trip down a dead end street!

The numbing aftermath of a failure may leave you feeling like you are sleep walking through life with no destination in particular, and certainly no joy! I am proof positive that there is life after; a life to be lived to the utmost—"The Utmost for His Highest," as author Oswald Chambers might say. It may be hard, or as in my case, it may take every ounce of energy you can muster!

I had a vision, the grandest kind,
Set a course. Sought the "secret find."
Gave my all, gave it heart and soul,
Never counted costs, saw enchanting goal.

Spent all my treasure as the years flew by,
Straining long, still another try.
Didn't take a tally, never saw as bad;
That dream took everything I had.

Once arrived, scanned the summit view,
Eyes full wide, but odd discontentment grew.
There must be more! *This can't be IT!*
Surely my calculations had been off a bit!

Then, as dawn pegged the scene as real;
Broke my heart, mocked the pointless zeal.
Body ached, mind bottomed, sad;
That *truth* took everything I had.

Frozen solid; jaded sight.
Floating lifeless, no will to fight.
Senseless, meaningless, all hope gone.
Gray skies! Gray matter! No light beyond!

'Til Jesus came and rocked me long,
Whispered love, the sweetest song.
Soothed my thoughts; my heart made glad!
To try again took everything I had.

His Spirit quickened; all things sprang new.
The tide was turning, flickering faith burned true.
Strength returning, the fog lifts at last!
Revealing purpose, "Will" screams, "Stand fast!"

No matter the weather, no matter the way!
No matter the darkness, or how bright shines the day!
His challenge given; my fortress glad.
Perfection's plan took everything I had!

COULD I DARE TO DREAM?

Sometimes life plays cruel tricks on us. The dreams that we give birth to in childhood, and that propel us into adolescence and beyond, can become life's greatest disappointments. If left unfulfilled, the grand dreams of youth evaporate before our eyes, even though we have put every ounce of energy towards bringing them to reality.

As days and years click by on the calendar and the heart-wrenching let down of unrealized dreams sinks in, it can give way to a self-protecting way of life; where we determine to never dream again. We wrongly conclude that such "vain imaginations" are child's play, and not the things on which to build our lives.

Besides, we tell ourselves, if we fail again, it would be too much to bear! So, we settle into living colorless lives devoid of disappointment, but too, the passionate pursuit of wild adventures. We convince ourselves that it is safer to live, and in a sense die, with nothing that stirs our minds or our hearts to ever hope beyond the mundane.

It was a season of this kind of despair that led me, in agony, to write this poem, which I dedicate to anyone who has had dreams that have been shattered.

Could I dare to shut my eyes,
And let the flinching cease?
Could the tension leave my jaws,
And leave my mind at peace?

Could I dare to trust the dark,
Release my tightened fist?
Could I relax, let go my hold;
Could "worry" *not* be missed?

Could I fight the learned distrust,
For all words, and thoughts, and deeds?
Could I dare hope to lay me down,
Minus thoughts that "fearing" breeds?

Could there be a sheltered spot,
To rest my weary head?
Could I awake and feel refreshed;
Have my spirit rise well fed?

Could I rest by waters still?
Could there be some shallow stream?
Could I ponder long on lilied bank?
Could I simply dare to DREAM!?

WITHOUT SPOT OR WRINKLE

This poem is a cry for the church, the bride of Christ, to seek revival. The words are the words of a bride who has been under attack, and left feeling abandoned and unworthy.

Christ came to bind up the brokenhearted, to proclaim freedom for the captive, and release the prisoners from darkness. We, Christ's bride, must redirect our efforts to prepare all believers for His soon return.

If Jesus is to come to the rescue,
To claim a pure bride for His own,
My prayer is, "Please do not tarry,
Your bride kneels at the altar alone!"

She's encountered relentless resistance,
Must admit it has taken a toll.
Abandoned white lace for "full camo!"
Had no choice, drawn her sword, on patrol!

Your bride is a mess there's no question,
Disheveled she toils long into night.
Filling mortar in bricks, patching breaches in walls,
Rebuild framing 'til plumb line's upright!

If your bride must have no spot or wrinkle,
She must be a sore sight to see.
Spattered mud on her veil no chance to call, "time!"
Can there be a "trump" sound reveille?

Not afforded the traditional entrance,
Not a dignified walk down the aisle.
She longs for her Champion to meet her!
Will her Groom look upon her and smile?

Oh! Your bride knows that she's to come purely,
Dreams to hear those sweet words, "You're complete!"
Trusting truth that her stains have been covered,
She drops burdens untold at His feet.

Without *love* there's no point to the struggle,
To stand firm on the Rock, and not fall!
Sure her Groom sees her heart and protects her,
Yields content! She has given her all!

Oh Jesus, Your bride cries, "Come quickly!"
With grace look upon her and say,
"Well done, faithful one; I've come for you,
Covered spot, not a wrinkle this day!"

A WHISTLE!

This poem was birthed after I heard a senior pastor speak to a group of young pastors at a luncheon. He encouraged them to create a special bond within their families so that the demands of shepherding a church congregation would not overshadow their homes and their hearts. After thinking of this sweet early morning ritual, I wrote this poem.

The pastor told a precious story,
Of His practice day by day.
To greet His bride with lilting notes,
Without words, His tender love for her, convey.

He whistles down the hall each morning,
Early with the light still dim.
His bride, with a smile, when she hears the tune,
Will whistle back to him.

'Tis the same in the realm of nature,
When a covey's flushed and flown.
Each feathered heart finds shelter,
Undercover in a place unknown.

When the danger's past then their daddy,
Will give a whistle to assure His own.
And the brood begins to assemble,
Toward His call and the rest of home.

Perhaps when Christ comes again to rule o'er us,
Long before blasting trumpets blare!
He may see fit to give a whistle first,
To ease a startled soul's despair.

With a cheer let His bride shout, "Good tidings!
Hear the call! (echo) Curra Hee!"
I will know without question where to find Him,
For His whistle is His call to me!

CASKETS OR COCOONS?

Could it be that the entire realm of our natural world has been designed by God as a testimony to the plan He had predestined for His Son Jesus' incarnation? (Romans 8:29)

Is it possible that all living things have been created with life cycles and instincts that point to Christ's handiwork? (Ephesians 2:10)

Could it also be, that God's plan for His Son serves as a metaphor for us; we, who have been created in His very image? (Genesis 1:27)

Though there may be, for us, seasons of darkness, despair and destruction, we can have hope that is birthed from and tethered to the promise of a resurrection. A new day! A new chance! A new life! (Romans 15:4)

Christ the purest sacrifice,
Redeemer purchased me.
Bore sin's weight for all the world,
To a cross on Calvary.

And there was nailed convicted,
Guilty verdict born for me.
Sentence harshest given,
Innocence died upon that tree.

Wrapped in finest linen,
Lord dipped in sweet perfume.
Then laid in borrowed sepulcher.
His casket? No. Cocoon!

For early on the third morn,
Christ arose to mock the dawn.
His matchless glory brilliant,
Testified sin's wage was gone!

The natural world bears witness,
And mirrors God's grand display.
Creation sowing seamless,
Repeats pattern day to day.

Begins the ugly duckling,
Comes then the graceful swan.
From wobbly knees to stallion,
Grand buck from speckled fawn.

A caterpillar's habit,
To spin on silken loom.
And cloak itself in darkness,
A casket? No. Cocoon!

For like our Heavenly Father,
It will rise again transformed.
The grub becomes a Monarch,
Brilliant wings! The worm reborn.

If some season burdens passion,
Causes light to winnow low.
If days drag on so dreary,
If all hope begins to go.

Remember that your Savior,
Has paid the debt complete.
That purpose still unspoken,
Does not define defeat.

If your instinct cries, "Find shelter!"
Lock all doors and lick the wound,
Retreat for your protection,
Building casket, or cocoon?

Gather all resources,
Find the power stored within.
And rise out of the ashes,
Build your strength! Begin again!

This life cannot defeat you,
Come forth from darkest tomb.
And rest upon His promise,
Escape casket! Burst cocoon!

IT IS FINISHED!

Easter is a very sacred time for Christians worldwide. To ponder a plan that would permit the Son of God to be offered up as a perfect sacrifice, for the establishment of a New Covenant, could not possibly have had its genesis in the mind of man.

It seems unfathomable to think that man would have ever had the instinct or courage to devise a plan that would include such a One to be given in exchange for the redemption all of mankind, for all time. God gave His only Son for us—an incomprehensible truth!

This plan had to have been created in the halls of heaven, (before Almighty God set this universe and time in motion) agreed to by His Son, and fulfilled precisely in "the fullness of time" as purposed by God on His kingdom calendar.

Then God, throughout history, commanded men to chronicle that plan, with Christ as the common and central thread woven thematically from the first page of the Book of Genesis to the last page of the Book of Revelation.

We, in earthly garb, cannot possibly imagine what the totality of the simple statement would encompass, the last words to be spoken by Christ from a cruel cross on a hill called Calvary, "It is finished!"

Rejoice! Three words so simply spoken,
Proclaimed from rugged cross, heartbroken!
Sealed indeed, none else needs done;
"Fear not!" the battle has been won.

No higher truth supplants Christ's word,
The Father's Son sent forth to gird –
The "who-so-evers" called to receive;
Then preach good news 'til all believe.

Man's highest thoughts trace God's own hand.
Matchless! Endless! Sub-atomic! Grand!
Still earth's great minds Christ does confound --
Let striving cease—claim higher ground!

Some new theory, next big plan;
Beware the folly to follow man.
Surely heaven's creation will build a throne,
And raise some mortal to enslave their own!

Edicts stone-etched from age to age,
Collapse, prove false, comes next great sage.
A dab of this, a pinch of that.
It's all the rage, then "new" falls flat.

Nirvana! Vapor! Sensual quest!
Man's search for self, less heaven's best;
Will come to naught, and leave men bare;
Drink the "poison," world's standard fare.

But He, the One, who spoke all conceived.
Offers freedom to all who believe.
Harkens, "Drop all weight that keeps you bound;
For in no other can your peace be found."

Missed the mark? Then turn from sin.
Find God's Truth. Begin again!
Christ came to set the captives free;
For such were some… but "chief-est" me!

Like me, if nothing else you've tried,
Has filled the hole that's deep inside.
There's hope that's found this side of grace;
Let go your hold, grant Christ His place.

Bitter! Vengeful! Long-held strife,
Gives way to peace! Fresh air! New life!
Christ said, "It's finished!" The promise won;
Rise from the ashes, thank God's own Son!

"It is finished!" Gone evil's host.
By grace through faith, lest one should boast.
"It's finished!" No addition! No take away!
He is the Truth; the Life; the Way!

"It is finished!" Take heed who hear;
Scoffers come who have no fear.
For He who sits enthroned above,
Proxies wrath as well as love!

We will not change the course that's laid,
"It's finished," proves the debt's been paid.
A simple fact! Yet how profound;
Through none but Christ, is salvation found.

SURRENDER OF AN ONLY SON

He is gone. The reality of the event will not leave me alone. He haunts me in a million little ways. I see his face staring back at me in the faces of toddlers, youngsters, and teenagers I pass during any given day, in any place where people gather.

Should they ever wonder why I have an odd look, as if I have seen a ghost; it is because—I have!

Their likeness to him can never be prepared for and always comes as a shock. They could never know that they are the spitting image of him in some bygone time. They are standing very much alive, but I see them as snapshots of memories. He was Nathan, as a little boy; or, he looks like Nathan did in grade school!

They breeze past me unsuspecting that they have conjured up in me another life; a life that exists frozen in time and, that can never be recaptured. It is done. Nathan's gone!

Grief is an overwhelming feeling. It can make you ache from head to toe, and just as swiftly cover you with a numbness and unbearable sense of loss that is truly indescribable—unless you've experienced it yourself.

I thank God that He has given us a hope that someday, somewhere in the future, all of the agony and pain will be no more, and we will see those we love again. No more tears, separation, or loss!

The expectation of life eternal carries me through each day knowing that this world is passing away and that there is a glorious life to come. Redeemed! Re-created! Restored! "One bright morning when this life is over, I'll fly away!"

Abraham in anguish,
Laid down while spirit groaned,
His precious son of promise,
The most treasured thing he owned.

His God had long been faithful,
His nature tested true.
Abe reasoned as he climbed that hill,
God, in time, makes all things new.

Hannah laid her heart bare,
As she wept at temple's door.
God's gracious answer given,
Came the son of her implore.

Dedicated to God's service,
His a voice to priest and king;
The child was given back to God,
Mother's fragrant offering.

Should a time on earth require,
An unthinkable exchange;
To lose the son long hoped for;
Cruelest plot life could arrange.

As light goes dark around you,
Heart and mind in drowning pain.
No place of peace or comfort,
No respite, or regain!

Could some solace come in knowing,
That in grief you're not alone?
Your GOD in heaven sees you;
Feels your ache and hears each moan.

He knows your pain in fullness,
For He too, had only one.
But offered up for all mankind,
The surrender of HIS Son.

Forever now connected;
God comforts those who mourn.
Shared loss brings sweetest Comrade;
Tender hearts forever torn.

One day we will pass over,
Eternal life has then begun.
Enduring bond in heaven,
He'll restore surrendered son.

Reflections on The 21st Century

BABBLE ON IN BABYLON

An observation and lament about the modern culture.

Brimming closets; shoe racks bulge.
One in every color! I'll just indulge.
My wildest whim will oft be met.
Bigger! Faster! Give me! Get!
No more boundaries, all fetters gone;
Travel on in Babylon.

May I go first? Knew you'd not care.
My time's precious, you've loads to spare.
I'll step in front, and off I'll go.
You see, I'm quite fast; and well, you're quite slow.
"I" and "me," fast friends; life-long.
Prattle on in Babylon.

Nip it here. Just there a lift.
I just turned forty. It was a gift!
The eyes, the lips, the bosom's new.
Sculpted, "lasered," injected too;
No wrinkles left, the tummy's gone,
Journey on in Babylon.

Enough of me. How do *you* view me?
You get one, but give me three!
I couldn't bear to just say, "No!"

It's my desire and rightly so;
Add another, and on, and on!
Shuffle on in Babylon.

No end in sight, which I can see.
Today's blocked by the mirror in front of me.
A wreck, a death, tsunami tide!
It mildly concerns me I must confide.
T.V. claims tens of thousands gone!
Oh well, let's see what else is on!
Numb to the sight of a brilliant dawn,
Sinking fast in Babylon.

Like a lobster in a pot, who begins to like the water hot,
I've been duped, been tricked, been "had!"
Convinced that truth is somehow bad,
Evil coddled, it cooed, and purred.
It beckoned me. It called. It lured!
Now in a place with the lights turned on.
I'm racing home from Babylon!

LOCKED UP OR DEAD!

The birth of this poem was a "shame on you" moment for me. I had just come through our church lobby which was full of kids, suitcases, and lots of noise. Kids seemed to be everywhere, all anxious to hit the road for the annual beach retreat, the signature event that ushered in summer at church.

I had never been to a beach retreat and I remember having a private conversation with the Lord that indicated that I had found Him without beach retreat, and had concluded that all the fanfare might be much ado about nothing. I recall, as those thoughts passed from my head to heaven, that a pang of reprimand had reverberated back to me, and I apologized to the Lord for my cynicism. The summer passed and I thought no more about the inappropriate comment.

Then came the church service that showed a recap of all the events for that year's retreat and my heart sank. A young man, probably about seventeen or eighteen, was being interviewed on camera and tearfully explained that the retreat had changed his life! He confessed how he had been going down the wrong path; and that beach retreat was a turning point for him.

He smiled and proclaimed that he had been forever changed at the beach. He said that had he not been invited, he wasn't sure where he would have ended up! Then he said these words that are forever seared in my memory. "I'd probably be locked up, (pause) or dead!"

"Oh no!" I thought. I felt sick at my stomach. An answer from heaven for fools like me, who question the methods of God's people who are trying by any means to make Jesus known to all people. The following poem came as a result of my struggle to move past the chastening I received for my insubordination.

His dark eyes welled, prompting downward gaze,
He shook his head, gave solemn praise,
To the One who bore his weight instead *confessing,*
"Without Him I'd be locked up... or dead!"

Seen too much bad in too few years,
Fighting tough, no time for tears.
Then came the One who comforted *claiming,*
"Without Him I'd be locked up... or dead!"

No protection, a childhood gone.
The battle raging dawn to dawn.
'Til he found the One called, "Heaven's Bread," *proclaiming,*
"Without Him I'd be locked up... or dead!"

Too young for memories stark and cruel,
Fanned by anger's flame, and bitter's fuel.
"Come unto to Me," was all He said, *knowing,*
"Without Him I'd be locked up... or dead!"

A warrior born from dark abyss.
The liar's foiled, his plan amiss.
Lost, yet found! No longer dread, *sensing*,
"Without Him I'd be locked up… or dead!"

Lord keep him close I humbly ask,
Prepare for him some mighty task.
Have him look to the hills, in power led, *remembering*,
"Without Him I'd be locked up… or dead!"

DO YOU HAVE FLOWERS?

The question was asked of a pastor who was visiting a dangerously dictatorial communist country. His communist hosts had been asking him questions about his life in America. They asked him how big his house was. How many families shared the house? Did he have children?

Then a question was asked by a five or six-year-old girl, who was not the least bit shy in the asking. To her, life was as simple as pretty flowers. I felt sure that in all the training and indoctrination that typifies this harsh culture that admiration for a flower would have been frowned upon as the quintessential example of frivolous activity reserved for western cultures that love to spend their time in pointless pursuits, wasting the precious time and resources of the "state." Yet, her question came from her heart; the yearning of a child who was captivated by the idea of a garden in one's own back yard.

The question posed by such innocence, buoyed my spirit in the knowledge that although tyranny's boots move ruthlessly throughout the captive world, God's divine grace and mercy still plant seeds of hope in the lives of those who, by all rights should not know Him! She had seen God's handiwork and longed for a garden of her own!

Kings may rise, and despots rule,
With twisted minds and hearts of stone;
And try to lift themselves on high,
But a little one asks, "Do you have flowers?"

Blind guides and fools exalt their thoughts,
And spew, "All life is happenstance;"
And crush the masses with iron fists.
But a little one asks, "Do you have flowers?"

"No God!" The mantra, the hedonistic cry.
"He's dead!" The credo of the neural trust.
"Some big bang!" The best and brightest guess,
But a child asks simply, "Do you have flowers?"

March in lock-step on some distant shore.
Question not, the wisdom from oppression's throne!
Your lot's the short stick, the die's been cast!
But a little one asks, "Do you have flowers?"

What glorious assurance God gives His own,
That He is, and we the apples of His eye.
No uniform, no flag, no gun can squash the spirit
Of a little one who asks, "Do you have flowers?"

Celebrate Him, or claim He is not real.
Close Him out, or up, or down! He bursts forth afresh.
His will is done, though some will never see it so.
Oh, for little ones asking, "Do you have flowers?"

Powerfully, His active hand, orchestrates with scalpel's touch.
We hear prophetic tongues long gone, "Bear the torch!
Light the path for us!"
He commands, "Fear not, I make all things new!

Yes, little one, He has flowers!"

FROM "SCRATCH!"

This is a whimsical look at the modern world. I wrote this poem as I listened to members of my family speak at the dinner table about an heirloom recipe for meat balls, that had been handed down from generation to generation by an Italian aunt.

As I listened to the list of ingredients, and the painstaking time it took to cook these spheres of perfection, I felt guilty about how little time I devoted to meal preparation in my own home. I could not fathom having the luxury of the time to create such sumptuous meatball treats, which is doubly troubling for my husband, who loves to eat!

Bless his heart. He long ago abandoned the dream that his wife would become the Julia Child of this age!

"Instant," the operative word for the day,
Be it oatmeal, pudding, or tea.
I'm not even sure that it's food we prepare;
At least, doesn't seem so to me.

Gone are the days we could boast of "homemade,"
Those cookies made batch after batch.
Eggs and sweet cream, made those gooey delights,
Alas, no one makes them "from scratch!"

Meals in five minutes, wedded microwave bliss,
With ingredients too complex to spell.
And we reach for the *Pepto* with nary a blink,
Discomfort with ease we dispel.

What happened to stews simmered long on the stove,
Or fish filleted fresh from the catch?
Or, yeast rolls raised twice, baked a golden-y brown?
No mistaking those smells were from "scratch!"

Now we have bok choy, and English snow peas,
And specialty pastas in sacks.
We buy eggs with no yolks, laid by free-ranging hens??
And we "supersize" fries and *Big Macs*®!

Long gone is the art of a pie crust with lard,
Now biscuits in rolls we detach.
And the jam that we smother, comes from the west coast.
It's a shame no one makes it from "scratch!"

So we forfeit aromas our sensory store,
And meals lose their savory charm.
And the kids have no memories that smells conjure up.
Are eggs laid by chickens on farms?!

We unwrap some nugget from the *Drive Thru Express,*
Long days between key in the latch.
Gone are the recipes honored and shared.
No time left to make it from "scratch!"

The vitamin craze has us popping odd pills,
To increase our vigor and vim.
And we try sugar-free, low-fat, and low-carb,
All out efforts to stay fit and trim.

They claim we've evolved; a superior lot!
Who me, grow a vegetable patch?
Rather lunch in a box, a can, or a pouch!
Makes no sense to just make it from "scratch!"

Meals with the family prepared with great care,
Are a thing of some by-gone day past.
Schedule's too frantic, not the time for a plan,
I'll stop to eat something, but "fast!"

There's homework, and housework, and the year-end report;
Folding laundry, and socks with no match.
How I'd love to smell cookies in my kitchen tonight,
Stir that mix, and pretend they're from "scratch!"

LAST ONE STANDING

There is an evil presence that roams this earth looking relentlessly for whom he might devour.

No matter what you call him, the evil one, the devil, Satan, or Lucifer, his modus operandi is to steal, to kill, and to destroy. These outcomes are his calling card. He delights in reigning havoc upon the children of God.

It is incumbent therefore, for those who are God's children, to become wise concerning his schemes, and to resist any destructive plot he has designed for us and those close to us.

Christ warned us of the characteristics of a demonic attack. So, to see evil's fingerprints on a life should trigger us to run for the cover that Christ provides us. He is our strength and high tower. An ever-present help in time of trouble, He is our banner of protection!

Satan moved early to claim that child,
Convinced her mind; chose a path gone wild!
She announced to all, "Gonna have a ball!"
So sure she'd be the last one standing.

Evil skulked, church doors open wide,
Stirred the pot; spawned a great divide.
Unseen dark force tried to steer a course,
O'er the edge, leaving no one standing.

Idle hands left too long alone,
Boiling anger, hatred raised full grown!
And in due time births a life of crime,
Not a thought to leave the last one standing.

Standard fare, Satan's soup-de-jour,
Preys on innocence. Fabricates to lure.
Truth is dead, misguided minds are led,
In error 'til there's no one standing.

Useful tools for an evil plot,
Fuel the soul, make it burning hot!
Unleash false plan, tell it man to man,
Satan's sure he'll be the last one standing.

Evil's battled long for the things of God,
To usurp His throne and to bear the rod.
Going to and fro, dealing blow on blow,
Delusion strong that he's the last one standing!

But...

The King of Kings, and Lord of Lords,
On fiery steed, with brandished sword;
Comes for His own, and ascends His throne.
No doubt, He'll be the last one standing!

IN SPITE OF...

What an unmistakably unmerited gift to have the forgiveness and mercy of Almighty God.

When I begin to take inventory of how underserving I am to be a recipient of God's leniency, it leaves me baffled. How could my worst moments, fueled by any number of excuses, not at some point disqualify me from God's considering me a child of His?

He should have given up on me years ago; and yet, He has not! I am forever grateful that, but for the grace of God, I would be alone and lost in this world. Thank God He found me--not perfect, but forgiven. Not where I need to be, but closer than I used to be!

> *"I count not myself to have apprehended: but this one thing I do, forgetting those things which are behind and reaching for those things which are before I press on toward the goal to win the prize for which God called me Heavenward in Christ Jesus"* (Phil. 3:13-14).

In spite of my obstinate demand for, "my way!"
And my cross-armed refusals birthed day after day.
In spite of my stubborn and arrogant flair,
I'm astonished *to think* Jesus loves me.

In spite of my split-seconded impassioned retorts,
Thinking all within ear-shot deserve my reports.
In spite of my penchant for records set straight,
I'm surprised *to think* Jesus loves me.

In spite of a heart spilling acid when bumped,
A temper on fire, and poor victims left stumped.
In spite of my self-imposed right to hold court,
I'm embarrassed *to think* Jesus loves me.

In spite of my callousness born of sheer pride.
No quarter, no mercy, nowhere you can hide.
In spite of a hollowed out view of His grace;
I'm frightened *to think* Jesus loves me.

In spite of the me who falls flat at His feet;
Acknowledging sin, and a life of defeat.
In spite of how little I deserve His first glance,
It's pure joy *to know* Jesus loves me!

HOWL AT THE MOON!

Life does not ever go precisely as we plan. Yet there can be, in us, a naïve expectation that if we are good, we will never know pain or defeat. We must understand that there is a time and a purpose for everything under heaven. It would be foolish for us to think that God will not ever allow dark times to come into our lives. Those times however, are not designed to destroy us, but rather, to build us up and transform us into the people God has called us to be.

Sometimes the darkest days end giving the brightest light; a light that creates wisdom and revelation that could not be acquired in any other way than by the dark valley road. Understanding that God is not trying to harm us, but is intent on molding and finishing us as He prescribes, is the key to weathering the storms that will inevitably come into all lives. We are to stand firm in the face of adversity and see what God has in store for those who love Him.

His way is meant to prosper, not to harm us; to create in us a hope for the future.

Big man on campus, the belle of the ball,
Sweeps us euphoric to heights ten feet tall.
Nary a thought past the lunch date at noon,
Giggling and giddy, we'll howl at the moon.

Some sophomoric view of just where we'll end up,
The life of the party, The President's Cup!
Demands for each day, deserved silver spoon,
Top Drawer's the new normal, and we'll howl at the moon.

'til somehow unnoticed there's a bump in the road,
The "Plan's" topsy-turvy, futilely kick at the goad.
This *does not* fit the schedule! Wail a sad tune!
Beat your chest and defiantly ... howl at the moon!

"Why is this hap'ning to me? It's not fair!"
"I have places to go, and no treasure to spare!"
"I did not choose *this* pathway! This detour's too soon!"
Red faced, with clenched fist, senselessly howl at the moon!

With all the strength one can muster, we stride hopelessly on,
No lilt in the gait, expectation all gone.
Forced introspection, temperate prayer softly croon;
Earnest praise given Author who created the moon.

No more self-direction, no more wasted time!
No self-promotion! Birthed. A new paradigm.
One built by Our Father—new life from dry dune.
With awed wonder and joy, reverently howl at the moon!

STAND DOWN!

(Benghazi through the eyes of John 15:13)

We may never know what happened in Benghazi, Libya that fateful night. But I marvel at the spirit of the brave American men and women who volunteer to fight for freedom all over the globe. Though the spirit that fuels them may be diverse, their sacrifice was defined centuries ago when Jesus spoke to His disciples giving them the ultimate illustration of love… <u>"That you lay down your life for another!"</u>

The battle raged beyond the gate,
The fire intense, the hour late!
From deep within the soul of man,
The urge to GO—*fight hand-to-hand!*

But comes the edict from higher Chain,
Command? "Sit still! You must remain!"
Torment boils, no rest is found,
Mind echoes the blasts, *"Stand down! Stand down!"*

Heart's alive! The mission clear.
Can't sit still! Resolute! No fear!
Battle's been drawn, *Go forth, engage!*
Highest call fuels RIGHT's outrage.

Chaos reigns, evil roams at large!
Remembered oath, "It is *my* charge!"
Makes no sense that from higher ground,
Comes cowards' voice, *"Stand down! Stand down!"*

Not for glory, nor for gain,
But simply LOVE can but explain;
How the soul of man, when given choice,
Puts self aside—gives TRUTH her voice.

Bursts from safety to engage cruel plan,
Sacrifice ALL for fellow man!
Regrets? Not one! Save that hollow sound,
From the foolish crowing *"Stand down! Stand down!"*

This IS the best of times, though worst,
When folly of man puts "worldly" first.
"Save the bacon!" "Save the cause!"
"Full speed ahead!" "No blink, no pause!"

Yet Divine spark proves not all is fate,
That GOOD endures, does NOT take the bait!
'Tis for freedom that Christ died for ALL!
His Spirit's alive to hear the call!

Our challenge remains from eons past,
To live for truth where right stands fast;
And throws aside what the world holds sound,
Stand up! Stand firm! But, NEVER *Stand Down!*

SNIPERS ON THOSE HILLS

I watched the television in disbelief as I saw agents of our federal government surround a rancher in the western part of our country; bringing the full weight of the government's judicial arm down on an American family.

As I listened to the news commentators I learned that federal employees, in military garb, armed with assault weapons were confronting family members and supporters at the front gate of the rancher's property, and had gone so far as to station snipers in the hills above that property.

My heart sank as I saw the events unfold. I contemplated what those brave souls who had first come to this country, would have thought, had they witnessed this confrontation in the 21st-century. I could not help but reflect on the historical circumstances that led to our country's founding, and the Christian tenants that were woven into our Constitution *and* Bill of Rights.

The earliest pilgrims were indisputably escaping centuries of religious persecution in Europe. It occurred to me that the fabric of our nation had been woven with the colors of a heavy-handed ruling authority, as well as Christian tenants of faith that were no doubt the impetus for such iconic statements as, "Give me liberty or give me death!"

The Bible boldly proclaims that man's freedom is given only by God, and that it is therefore not to be bartered or bullied away by any earthly entity. This is the spirit that birthed a brave Scot, William Wallace, who, when faced with an encroaching English power, ran counter to the culture and claimed, until the guillotine's blade silenced him, "FREEDOM!"

This poem is a pondering of how this country began and ultimately where we are heading as outlined by God in His Word.

They left their lands of tyranny,
With nothing but a dream.
To worship free in far 'way place,
Glimpsed a promise yet unseen.

And though there were no guarantees,
New land would better be.
Sound reason rang through every thread,
Chimed, "Escape brutality!"

So they ventured forth upon high seas;
Sailed west on ocean's tide.
A solemn choice, not fanciful,
There was nowhere left to hide.

And so to Plymouth Rock – by grace,
Through faith that fueled their wills.
Never dreaming in their wildest,
A time with snipers on those hills.

And they almost died the first year;
Then made it barely passed next spring.
With patient toil the land bore fruit,
A fragrant offering.

Divinely given blessing,
Freedom's gift began to bloom;
And beckoned huddled masses,
Past Lady's torch in harbor's womb!

First taste of sweetest freedom,
Sparks new life in mortal souls.
The guiding hand from Heaven,
Advanced most noble goals.

But from the one doomed to fiery lake,
Snake's seething anger spills.
His pledge? *To stop their purposes!*
He'd put snipers on those hills.

And pastors planted churches,
Taught the Way, the Truth, the Life.
Birthed Ivy League's high learning;
Hallowed halls devoid of strife.

Heaven's wisdom raining favor,
Guided faithful through the fray;
And hope sprang forth eternal,
Growing leaps and bounds by day.

Good never dwelled suspecting,
That an evil could take hold;
And supplant the purest motives,
With a "modus" known from old.

Screeching! Scratching! Clawing!
Unguarded hearts hell's poison fills.
'Ole serpent slinks the backstreets,
Stations snipers on those hills.

God's Word the truest roadmap!
His inspiration fueled their way.
Came 'lectric lights and telephones,
Wilbur's flight would change the day.

God's divine spark led His faithful;
Reaped the bounty fine reward!
Times of peace would follow,
Plowshares soon replaced the sword.

But somewhere in blessing's progress,
There became a clouded view.
"Absolutes" now deemed tainted,
Misguided theories grew and grew.

Good men had built foundations strong,
Honed too, their weapon skills,
Divine knowing long war 'gainst them,
Would bring snipers to those hills.

Now evil's tearing down those fences;
That for generations stood.
Have sold recycled rhetoric,
Blackest lies, replacing good.

So as with all earth's kingdoms,
That stood in God's appointed hour;
We've sacrificed our freedom,
Tragic price to gain cruel power.

"Experience," now the teacher,
We will live forefathers' fate;
And walk those hellish hallways,
For we cannot shut the gate.

The devil's commandeered the courthouse,
Captured children sent to school!
"Indoctrinate!" the mandate.
"Elevate the common fool!"

The wicked have no knowing,
They were marked 'fore time began;
And will one day meet their Maker!
With ALL power to foil their plan.

Christ, the Heir of all things sacred!
Treads the winepress of His ire!
And when timing reaches fullness,
He'll fight fire with *holy fire!*

He will rise from at the right hand,
Mount white steed at trumpet's sound.
With chosen, faithful follow'rs,
He'll reclaim all stolen ground!

And in that grand finale,
A battle of the wills;
There is no doubt that Truth wins out,
Vanquished snipers lose those hills!

THE HEARTLAND

I was sitting on a bench outside the S&S Automotive Shop in an east Texas town. Our old SUV, affectionately nicknamed "White Thunder" by my husband, was having some air conditioning repair done, and I was passing the time sitting in front of the business until "Ole Thunder" was blowing cool again.

As I sat, I marveled at the commerce I saw pass before me through the only traffic light in town. There were flatbed trucks carrying fresh cut timber, extended-cab pickups hauling hay, and trailer tractors outfitted with bush hogs and hay forks coming and going in orchestrated succession.

I am a city girl, and the introduction to country life as a baby boomer has opened up a fresh new world to me; a world that up until recently, I was blissfully unaware existed. I now know it exists in rural communities across America.

This poem is dedicated to all those hardy souls who plant and harvest, who fix and are "fixin' to;" whose love of family and country are never hard to discern; and to whom blue jean coveralls and denim shirts are the uniform of the day.

This writing is to acknowledge fondly all those who comprise the *farms, ranches, machine shops, welding depots, and builders' warehouses all over this great land. Kudos from a city slicker who does not know "come here" from "sic 'em!"*

Feed stores and hay barns,
And respect for "Old Glory;"
Backbones and "Yes ma'ams,"
Tell more of the story.

Bushels and round bales;
Earnest sweat from a brow;
Where "Heifer" and "steer,"
Describe more than just "cow!"

Clearing of land and,
Grinding down stumps;
Leathered faces and hands,
And nicknames like "Grumps."

Hats taken off,
Heads bowed to give thanks.
Good times and laughter,
And endearing pranks.

Deals sealed with a handshake,
Look you square in the eye.
Hot dogs and sparklers,
On the 4th of July.

Home grown tomatoes,
Pickled okra spiced right,
Recipe heirlooms,
Handed down with delight.

Friends gathered like treasure,
Wisely view what to keep.
Crickets and tree frogs,
Lulling children to sleep.

Fire flies and bonfires,
And marshmallow roasts,
Birth stories of fairies,
And white knights, and ghosts.

Nurtured in nature,
Lessons learned in plain sight.
Prayers said by the bedside;
Then turn out the light.

Fresh air and stillness;
A pause to take stock.
Time measured in fullness, not
The tick of a clock.

No lure of the bright lights,
Can tempt folks like these.
Grounded and rooted,
Unimpressed by degrees.

Keen knowing a peace that,
No price tag can sway.
Rather lift rod in a pond,
At the end of a day.

Many the town,
And the folk seen therein;
Who greet with a nod, tip of hat,
Or a grin.

What the world holds as precious,
They see as "fools' gold."
Not impressed by what sparkles,
No matter how it's been sold.

Gathering to worship,
Is still in their vogue.
Offering prayers for sure guidance,
At each fork in The road.

This is The Heartbeat,
Of a nation still found,
In backwoods, and off roads;
Planting God's fertile ground.

These folk hear the call,
|To be fruitful and bloom;
And pine not for bow ties,
Or some cubical tomb.

"Beamers" and "roadsters,"
Are deemed useless to these.
John Deere front end loader,
Is their choice, if you please.

They're proudly just country,
As sweet apple pie.
Love of family and freedom,
Solemn truths to live by.

These know without question,
Make a purposeful stand;
To forfeit the fluff,
To guard and groom the Heartland.

For more about the author go to:

www.FairwayMinistries.com

www.ingramcontent.com/pod-product-compliance
Lightning Source LLC
Chambersburg PA
CBHW070119080526
44586CB00013B/1333